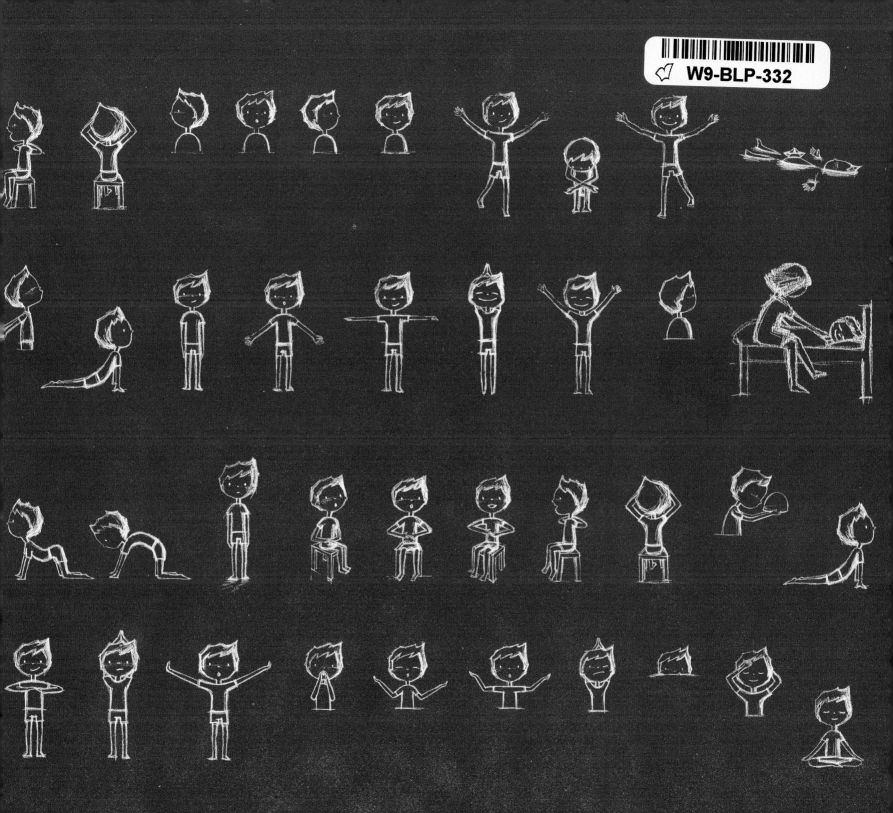

W9-BLP-332

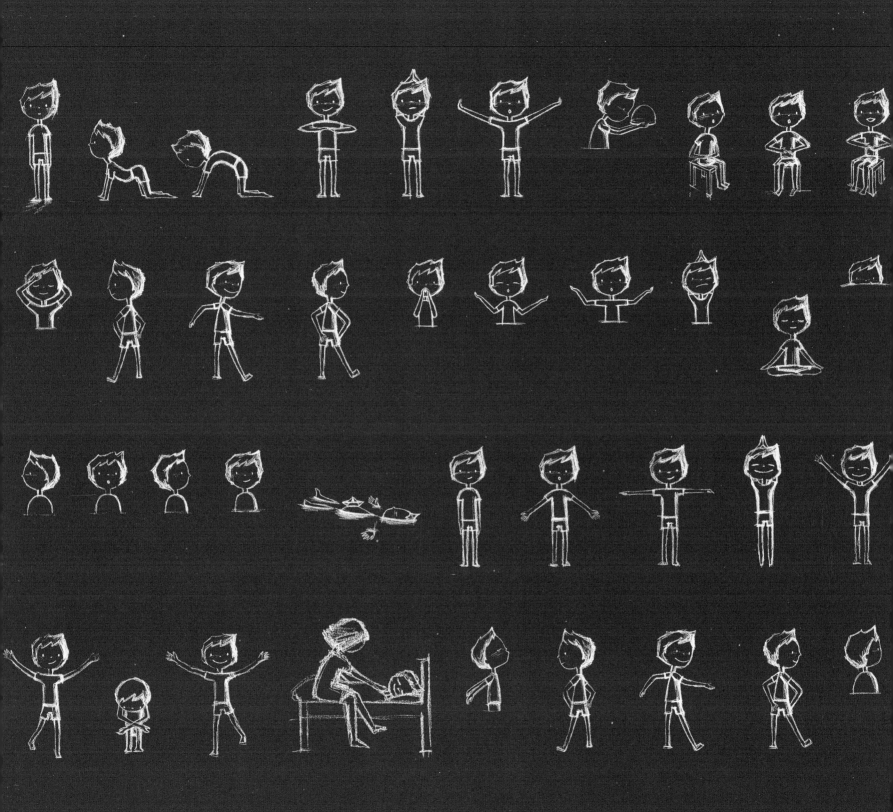

BREATHE

© 2015 Inês Castel-Branco
Original title: "Respira" Published for the first time in 2015 in Spain by Fragmenta Editorial
Published by agreement with Fragmenta Editorial through the VeroK Agency, Barcelona, Spain

English translation copyright © 2018 by Magination Press, an imprint of the American Psychological Association. All rights reserved. Except as permitted under the United States Copyright Act of 1976, no part of this publication may be reproduced or distributed in any form or by any means, or stored in a database or retrieval system, without the prior written permission of the publisher.

Published by
MAGINATION PRESS®
American Psychological Association
750 First Street NE
Washington, DC 20002

Magination Press is a registered trademark of the American Psychological Association.
For more information about our books, including a complete catalog, please write to us, call 1-800-374-2721, or visit our website at www.apa.org/pubs/magination.

English translation by Jenna Miley and Katie ten Hagen
Book design by Gwen Grafft

Printed by Lake Book Manufacturing, Inc., Melrose Park, IL

Library of Congress Cataloging-in-Publication Data
Names: Castel-Branco, Inês, 1977- author.
Title: Breathe / by Inês Castel-Branco.
Other titles: Respira. English
Description: Washington, DC : Magination Press, American Psychological Association, [2018] |
    Audience: Age 4-8. | Originally published in Catalan and Spanish as Respira by Fragmenta (Spain),
    text and illustrations copyright © 2015 by Inês Castel-Branco. | English translation by Jenna Miley
    and Katie ten Hagen.
Identifiers: LCCN 2017040492| ISBN 9781433828720 (hardcover) | ISBN 1433828723 (hardcover)
Subjects: LCSH: Breathing exercises—Juvenile literature. | Respiration—Juvenile literature.
Classification: LCC RM733 .C37 2018 | DDC 615.8/36--dc23 LC record available at https://lccn.loc.gov/2017040492

Manufactured in the United States of America
10 9 8 7 6 5 4 3 2 1

To Francesc, Anna, and Miquel, with whom I have practiced all of these exercises—IC-B

OCT 2 9 2018

BREATHE

by INÊS CASTEL-BRANCO

Magination Press • Washington, DC • American Psychological Association

OCT 2 9 2018

"Mom, I can't sleep!"

"Why not?"

"I don't know…I'm nervous and I can't stop thinking, thinking, thinking…"

"Do you want me to teach you how to breathe?"

"Breathe? But I already know how to breathe!"

"But have you ever stopped to see how you do it? Where the air comes in and out? If it fills more of your belly or your chest? If you are doing it slowly or quickly?"

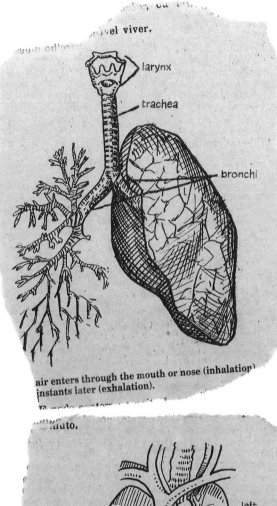

air enters through the mouth or nose (inhalation) instants later (exhalation).

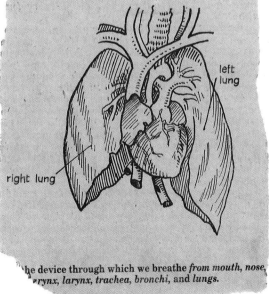

he device through which we breathe *from mouth, nose, rynx, larynx, trachea, bronchi, and lungs.*

"Let's make a paper boat and put it on your belly."

"A boat? OK, I can make one!"

"Now imagine this boat is sailing in the ocean—it goes up when the air fills your tummy as you breathe in, and it goes down as you breathe out."

"Breathing in…and breathing out."

"You are like a wave in the sea. You are not in a rush. Let yourself go and follow the gentle movement, and the rhythm of your breathing will become slower."

"Now you have worked with the lower part of your lungs, but you can also breathe with the middle part."

"To fill my chest with air?"

"Yes! You'll see how much comes in. Imagine that you take a balloon in your hands and fill it up. The balloon keeps getting bigger and bigger…"

EXHALE

INHALE

1

2

"Oh, it popped! I'll try again!"

"You can breathe in slowly and imagine that you're smelling a rose…"

"…or lavender, or mint…"

"…a pine tree, or the sea…"

"…or wet soil after a storm."

"Did you know that your arms can help you breathe with the upper part of your lungs?"

"Really?"

"Let's try it…do you want to be a rocket that goes up into the sky?"

BAAAMMMM

"Up to other galaxies?"

"Very far away! Put your hands together and bring them up very high, count up to five, and after take-off bring them down on your sides in a cloud of smoke."

"Have you felt how you can breathe with the different parts of your lungs?"

"Yes! But what if I want to breathe with all of the parts?"

"You can imagine that you are a tree, a tree that is growing."

"My feet are the roots, my body the trunk…"

1 inhale
exhale

2

"With each breath, you bring your arms up, up, up, opening the chest. After three breaths, draw a big circle, or even better, a very leafy treetop!"

"Full of leaves and red apples!"

"And with one big exhale, bring your arms down again and relax."

nhale
exhale

3 inhale

exhale

LA Editorial de Música BOIL
publicado y viene publicand
tales obras de estudio y conc
románticos y modernos, hecha
pedagogos musicales de Europa
prefacios e indicaciones técnicas
ideas de sus autores y, por co
que son objeto de estudios po
Esta casa lleva ya public
Alió, Bach, Beetho
ller, Chopin, Cleme
ny, Diabelli, Dusse
Händel, Haydn, H
Kohler, Kulhau, Ku
Liszt, Mendelssohn
Pischna, Quidant, R
mitt, Schubert, Sch
etc., las cuales constituy
Conservatorios y Acade

"I really enjoyed being a tree. And now…could I be an animal?"

"Let's see…how about an owl?"

"Yes! Did you know that they can't move their eyes?"

"So spin your head like they do. Breathe in while you look to each side, and breathe out when you bring your head back to the front."

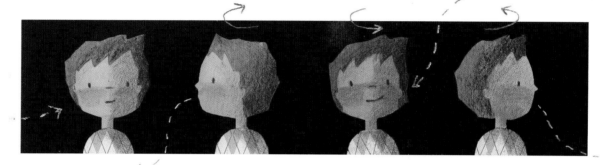

"You can also try to imitate a cat. What does a cat do?"

"It stretches out lazily…"

"Try it! Then arch your back, too. Breathe in while looking up, and breathe out while looking at the floor."

"To help stretch your back, you can also imagine you are a cobra…"

"The venomous snakes that lift their heads up to attack?"

"Exactly! Lie on the floor, and as you breathe in quietly, lift your body and your head up, leaning on your hands. Breathe out as you go down."

"And what if I want to fly?"

"You can be a crane that takes off on its flight very lightly. Balance on one foot first, then on the other, while you spread your wings out with elegance."

"It's hard to move like this!"

"You can do it! Breathe in when you fly, and breathe out when you bring your arms down and to the front."

"It's hard to loosen my back!"

"Alright, stand up and imagine you are a bell. Swing your arms from side to side."

"Ding-dong…"

"Breathe out with each chime as you twist your body. Let your body be completely flexible…"

"So that the bell rings, right?"

DING

DONG

DING DONG

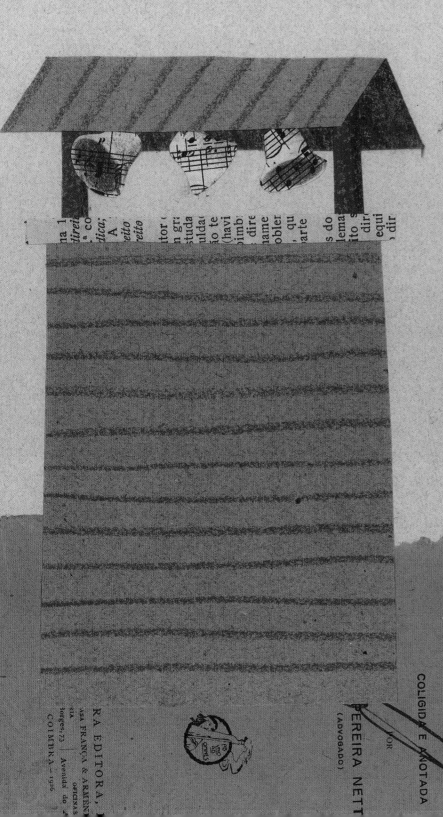

"Yes. When bell stops moving and goes quiet, place your palms on the front and back of your head. Calm down and concentrate while you gently breathe."

"Sometimes, to breathe well, it's helpful to imagine a geometric shape like a square, a triangle, some stairs, or a high wall."

"Or a mountain chain?"

"That's it! Relax while you trace the line of mountains with your mind. Breathe in as you climb to the top, and breathe out as you go down to the valley."

"Did you know that you can also breathe with letters? Every sound makes a different part of your body vibrate."

"They're not all the same?"

"No!"

"The letter O strengthens the heart."

"The letter U echoes in the belly."

"The letter E makes the
neck vibrate."

"The letter I brings
life to the head."

"The letter A clears the lungs."

shame
discouragement
anger
hate
envy
pain
anxiety
violence
sadness

"This all sounds nice, but there are still so many things that scare me!"

"They feel like storm clouds that keep you from seeing the sky, right?"

"Yes. How can I push them aside?"

"Imagine that each one of those fears is like a dark cloud. Then you take a deep breath and blow, blow, blow. Feel the fears go away, giving way to a blue sky."

"When you are feeling nervous, your body is like a snow globe that's been shaken."

"All the glitter is fluttering around just like the thoughts in my head."

"What happens to the glitter when you start to breathe deeply and hold the globe still?"

"It falls slowly down, until it reaches the bottom."

"Yes. The water becomes clear and the glitter settles down, just like your thoughts inside of you, if you know how to calm down."

BREATHE

"Now I've shown you lots of ways that moving and stretching your body can help you breathe. Imagining mountains or animals, blowing balloons or sailing boats, smelling roses or ringing bells, launching rockets or growing like a tree…"

"Thank you, Mom! Now I feel lighter than a cloud and not so heavy. I have more space inside."

"There you go! You found your inner space just by breathing! Do these exercises any time you feel nervous during the day. Pay attention, for a moment, to the air that comes in and out as you breathe."

"Thank you for everything you've helped me discover. I am very tired now."

"Come on, go back to bed now. You'll sleep well tonight."

BREATHE

Note to Parents & Caregivers

BREATHE is a conversation between a child and his mother at bedtime, but this interaction can happen any time or place. This book presents a compilation of exercises that can help little ones become aware of their breath.

And why is it important to know how to breathe well? If breathing is an innate physiological act for every human being, then we shouldn't worry about how we do it! When we think about a baby sleeping, we realize that her entire body breathes—her belly moves with each inhalation and exhalation. But, over the years, we lose that abdominal and complete breathing, the diaphragm begins to weaken, and we progress to a shallower breathing rhythm. Regaining a full breathing pattern is a very important step in reconnecting with our bodies. If children learn how to do it when they are young, they have an important tool for living more deeply, from the simplest and most necessary act that we all do—breathing. Since this theory seems very complicated and children love stories, *Breathe* presents a series of exercises—some come from yoga, tai chi, chi kung, or kinesiology—illustrated and adapted for children as they are already being applied in many schools and communities. In different religious traditions, there has always been a lot of importance given to the air we breathe, and the sacred has often been represented as the breath, the wind, the blowing spirit, the vital energy, etc. The practice of conscious meditation, centered on the breath and with the goal of being "present" in each moment, is called mindfulness.

In the educational field, there has been talk for years of the need to work on mindfulness with students in the face of the stresses of the current world. It's not just about trying techniques, but using them to learn to look inward, reflect, and be silent. In short, to live more open to oneself, to others, and to the world.

However, many families don't know how to do this at home. Traditions that made sense in the past have been lost and, often, nothing has appeared to replace them. The large amount of technological stimuli also does not help calm the mind at the end of the day. Taking deep, circular breaths creates an interior climate that one can build on in many ways: thanking the day, recalling special moments, or praying, in accordance with the beliefs of each family. It is not necessary to devote much time to it; it is only necessary to connect with the body, which takes us to the here and now while we inhale and exhale calmly.

Mother and Son

Breathing is directly related to our emotions. When we are nervous, our breathing is fast and noisy. When we are calm, it becomes slow and harmonious. In tense moments, if we know how to control breathing, we can react with serenity. How often do we want to calm ourselves but do not know how to do it? How often do we want to concentrate but have a thousand ideas racing around our head? How often do we want to sleep but the stress of tomorrow consumes our thoughts?

Exercise: We can observe the breath without intervening, simply feeling how the air enters and leaves the nostrils (or the mouth). When we focus on the act of breathing, we stop thinking about the thousand and one things that go through our heads at all times. In the belly and the chest there are no emotions or thoughts: only the air that enters and leaves, and fantastic organs fulfilling their mission.

Ocean Waves

This exercise helps to work abdominal breathing, which we all used during the first years of life. Yoga attaches great importance to breathing; *Pranayamas* are exercises to regulate vital energy (*prana*) through breathing. Water is a symbol of purification and of destruction of the negative. Feeling like a wave in the sea allows us to calm the respiratory rhythm and think about how we belong to a larger whole.

Exercise: The child stretches with their back on the floor, their eyes closed, and their arms relaxed beside their body. Place a paper or toy boat on their belly and encourage them to imagine they are a wave in the sea. The child can put one hand on the belly and another on the chest, to make sure that the belly moves and not the chest. By doing this, the air reaches the lower part of the lungs, expanding the diaphragm. When the child exhales, it is as if the air were absorbed inside and the belly deflates.

Blowing Up Balloons

This exercise creates the need for a deep breath, to blow forcefully and fill up an imaginary balloon. In doing this, the respiratory organs are relaxed and the lung capacity is increased. When the arms extend, the ribs separate and more space is created in the middle part of the lungs so that air can enter. Visualizing a balloon also allows you to think of the lungs like a balloon that swells and flattens.

Exercise: The child touches the corresponding fingers of each hand in front of their mouth, as if they had a balloon in the middle, and makes the first inhalation and exhalation. Then they separate them a bit and make the second. The third one takes place with the arms more open...until the imaginary balloon explodes and the child says "POP!" They need to take another "balloon" out of their pocket and start over. After repeating the exercise several times, you can tie the last imaginary balloon to an imaginary thread, let it fly through the sky, and wish it well it as it disappears.

Smell the Roses

The practice of smelling different scents uses olfactory evocations to achieve calm and fluid breathing. The child should imagine a smell that they know well, and inhale through the nose as slowly as they can to open all the pores of the bronchi and the lungs. When they exhale through the mouth, it is as if they are returning the scent to its place of origin. It is an exercise that works the imagination and the senses (a scent is usually associated with a color, a tactile sensation, or a taste).

Exercise: The child closes their eyes and imagines different smells that they know and enjoy. The inhalation and the exhalation must be paused. For maximum relaxation, the length of exhalation should be twice the length of inhalation, with a pause in between—there is even a specific "4-7-8" technique to fall asleep (4 seconds for inhalation, 7 seconds for a pause, and 8 seconds of exhalation). They can also, at the time of exhalation, imagine that they have to blow on a candle without putting it out; or scatter all the tufts of a dandelion; or make hundreds of soap bubbles; or fog up a glass window to draw on it...

Launch the Rocket

In this exercise, the child will imagine that they are a rocket that is preparing to go to the moon or a faraway planet. The movement of slowly stretching the arms upwards helps them to feel the verticality and dilate the thoracic cavity, allowing greater air intake in the lungs. The pause that happens with the arms up, while retaining the air, slows the respiratory rate and induces

serenity. Dropping the arms to the sides facilitates the closure of the space between the ribs and helps empty the lungs.

Exercise: The child is standing, their arms bent at the height of their shoulders and fingers touching each other in front of their chest. While inhaling, they put their palms together and lift them over their head, stretching their arms up as far as they can. Count up to five for the child to stand for a moment in this position. Then the rocket takes off with a cloud of smoke! The arms are pulled away, down to the sides, with the fingers of the hands facing upwards.

The Growing Tree

There are many versions of the tree that grows, some more complicated than the one presented here, but all of them focus on taking a full breath. The origin of this exercise is found in Egyptian yoga. As the arms rise on the sides, the chest opens and the air can occupy the entire interior space. The breath happens, then, from the abdomen to the lungs to the clavicle, so that we end up breathing with the totality of the lungs.

Exercise: Standing, with the feet forward, the knees slightly flexed and the arms on the side of the body, the child inhales while lifting their arms a little by their sides, and exhales in the same position. Then they inhale again as they raise their arms to shoulder height, and exhale again. Finally, they raise their arms all the way up and then, while exhaling, draw a big circle with their arms by

returning them to the starting position. Other variants begin in more closed positions to force an abdominal respiration.

The Owl and the Cat

These stretches are similar to those that athletes or dancers use to warm up. First is the owl's breathing, which helps reduce stress in the shoulders and stretch the neck. This exercise, in particular, helps to recondition the body, avoid stiff necks, and release tensions, as well as increase blood flow to the brain. The cat's position is a typical *asana* of yoga (called *Bidalasana*) that increases the flexibility of the back and stretches the muscles of the neck. By bending your back up, more space is created in the lungs; and by rounding it down, the chest closes and the lungs empty. This position can help you gain more physical flexibility.

Exercises: For the owl's exercise, the child sits with their back straight and begins to inhale, then exhales while turning their head to the right. They inhale again while they return their head to the center, then exhale and turn to the other side. They can place their right hand on their left shoulder when they look to the left, and their left hand over their right shoulder when they look to the right. To perform the exercise of the cat, the child is on their hands and knees with their hands resting on the floor, their back straight, and their head down. When they inhale, they raise their head and look upwards, arcing their back into a U-shape. With each exhalation, they hide their head, tucking their chin to their chest and arcing their back like a bridge.

The Cobra and the Crane

The cobra position (*Bhujangasana*) comes from yoga. Similar to the exercise of the cat, it also works the flexibility of the spinal column by strengthening the muscles. The snake that slithers through the grass and raises its head to look around can symbolize the awareness of one who is open to the world and is attentive to what is happening all around. The exercise of the crane belongs to the practice of *chi kung*, which means "Life Energy Cultivation," (where breath is a major component of the idea of "Life Energy") and more specifically to the practice of the Five Animals (Tiger, Deer, Monkey, Bear, and Crane), which is inspired by ancient shamanic practices.

Exercises: The child lies down with their belly on the floor and hands next to their shoulders. They inhale as they raise their head, extend their arms, and arch their back, then exhale while slowly returning to the starting position. This exercise can also be done with the child sitting at a table, with their hands and head resting on the table top. For the crane exercise, the child, standing, steps forward with their left foot, raises the heel of the right foot from the ground, and opens their hands by their sides like wings as they inhale. Then, as they exhale, they step forward with their right foot and bend over a little, crossing their hands in front of their knees. They can alternate both feet and walk forward, simulating the serene flight of this great and elegant bird.

Ring the Bells

The exercise of ringing the bell comes from a warm-up movement characteristic of *tai chi*, an ancient form of Chinese martial art that can be defined as the practice of "meditation in movement." This warm-up exercise uses a rotation to flex the spine, loosen the hips, and relax the entire body's muscles. The second exercise comes from kinesiology, which originates in traditional Chinese medicine (acupuncture in particular). The child puts one hand on their forehead and the other behind their head, closing their eyes and breathing serenely. Placing the hands in this position helps to draw attention to one's thoughts, which can aid in quieting and relaxing the mind.

Exercises: The child stands up, with legs apart, feet parallel, and knees slightly bent. They raise their arms as they inhale, and then drop them to each side, hitting the body and turning their hips while exhaling. They can also incorporate the neck and shoulders. To help balance the body, they should lift the tip of the foot towards where their arms are turned and stretch their leg in that direction. In the second position, from kinesiology, the child closes their eyes and places a hand on their forehead and another on the nape of their neck, while breathing calmly. There are other similar exercises that also help to focus and release tensions. For example, putting the fingers of both hands on the forehead, just above the eyes, can be used in much the same way.

Breathe With the Mountains

In this exercise, the mountains are a symbol (or *yantra*, in many Eastern ideologies, particularly tantric practices from India) that helps the mind to concentrate and better connect with the breath. We can use geometric figures,

such as squares, circles, and triangles, or other visuals like stairs, walls, mountains, numbers, or letters.

Exercise: You can draw a figure for the child to look at. Then explain how they have to "travel" this figure with their breath. In the case of a mountain range, for example, they follow the mountains' lines, inhaling each time they "climb" to a top and exhaling as they descend to the valley.

Vibrate With the Vowels

Sounds can help us to better feel our breath. The letters, in particular, might vibrate in different parts of the body and feel distinct from each other. It can be very centering to notice how these different sounds affect us uniquely.

Exercise: The child sits in a chair. Then they inhale deeply, and during the exhalation each vowel is drawn out with a constant tone, trying to notice the place of vibration: U (belly), O (heart), A (chest), E (neck) and I (head). The child can also breathe with consonants that offer more resistance to the exit of the air: the wind (ffffff...), a hose (shshshshsh...), a fan (vvvvvvv...) or a snake (ssssss...).

Blow Away the Clouds

This visualization aims to achieve a deep and rhythmic breathing, concentrating on oneself and abandoning negative thoughts. Since ancient times, visualizations have been used to induce relaxation or to imagine future situations and prepare a calm and positive response. But it's not just about imagining things or situations, but contemplating them consciously, creating them in our minds and allowing ourselves to transform.

Exercise: The child imagines a stormy sky and can name those dark clouds: fear, pain, shame, anger, envy, discouragement, etc. They will blow and imagine how the words are dispersed, the letters falling one by one until a blue sky appears. Another version is to inhale good words and to exhale their opposite: peace enters, war exits; love comes in, hate goes away; joy comes in, sadness leaves; trust comes in, fear goes out.

The Calming Jar

This exercise is a contemplation of the movements of the pieces of glitter or "snow" inside of a snow globe. The snow globe is a metaphor for our mind when we are trying to calm our swirling thoughts and feelings. When the glitter settles completely, the water is clear, and there is serenity.

Exercise: You can build a "snow globe" at home from a glass jar, water (distilled, if you can), a little glycerin (to give viscosity), and glitter. You can attach a figure to the inside of the lid (with silicone or glue) if you like, and then seal the lid on the jar. In times of commotion or emotional distress, the child can go to their room, shake the bottle, and observe how eventually the glitter settles and the water becomes clear.

Meditation

In this last exercise there are elements of all the previous ones; these are possible strategies (among many others) to help breathe, calm down, be present, control emotions, dispel fears, contemplate, give thanks, etc. All are tools that are accessible to children, games that they themselves want to experience and which will gradually transform them.

Exercise: In times of nervousness, fear, etc., breathe together. Take three or four full, deep breaths. Just a few breaths are enough to calm the rhythm of the body and change the mental state. Afterwards, ask your child how they feel. They are sure to surprise you...

About the Author & Illustrator

Inês Castel-Branco was born in Lisbon and lived for many years in a small city in the interior of Portugal that shares her name: Castelo Branco. She loved to play the piano. She also spent many vacations drawing in a notepad, discovering her own distinct methods of painting, and learning to take photos with her father's antique Canon. At 18 years old, she went to study architecture in Oporto (also in Portugal). Later, curiosity led her to study abroad in Barcelona, Spain. It was only supposed to be for a year, but she liked the city so much that she stayed another year to do a master's degree, then a doctorate, and wound up doing a thesis on the theatre of the '60s. During all of this, she decided to found Fragmenta Editorial with Ignasi Moreta, and so submerged herself in the fascinating world of the typography and layout of books. With the birth of their three children, Inês returned to making models (now of castles, zoos, doll houses…), and they discovered the marvels that can be made with recycled objects (which are explained on Inês's blog, "Mamá recicla"). Their love of children's books also grew, until they decided to start this collection. One morning, during breakfast, she "saw" in her mind the book that you now have in your hands, and she once again took up her brushes and painted.

About Magination Press

Magination Press is an imprint of the American Psychological Association, the largest scientific and professional organization representing psychologists in the United States and the largest association of psychologists worldwide.

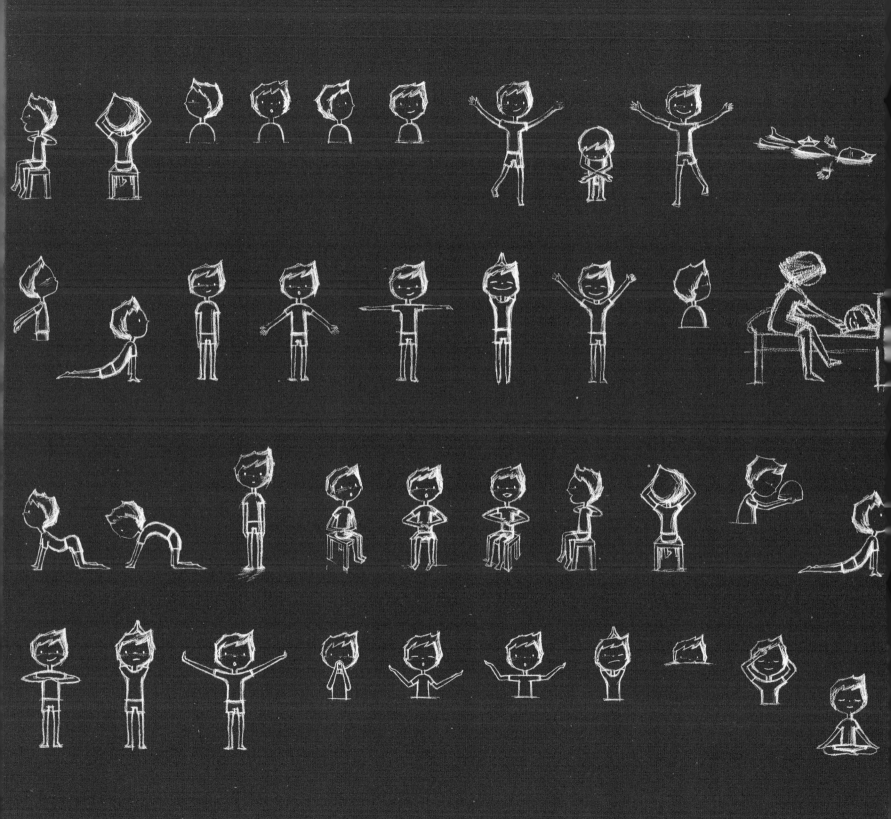

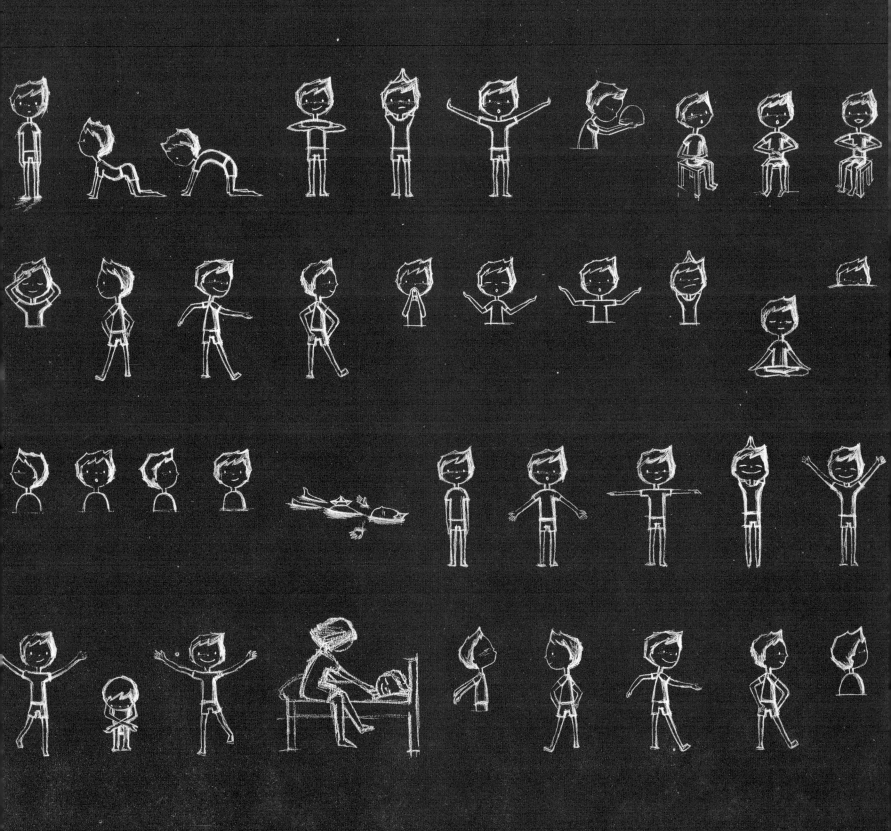